Twin Talk

PETER C HEASLIP

Methuen Children's Books

Imran and Qadir are twins.

They look the same and they sleep in the same bed.

And sometimes they play tricks on each other.

"I have a plan," said Imran.

"Tomorrow is Saturday and I'm going to speak Urdu all day."

"If you speak Urdu I'll speak English," said Qadir.

In the morning their mum came in to wake them up and to give them their clean shirts.

"It's time to get up," she said.

"Good morning," said Qadir.

"Salām alakum," said Imran.

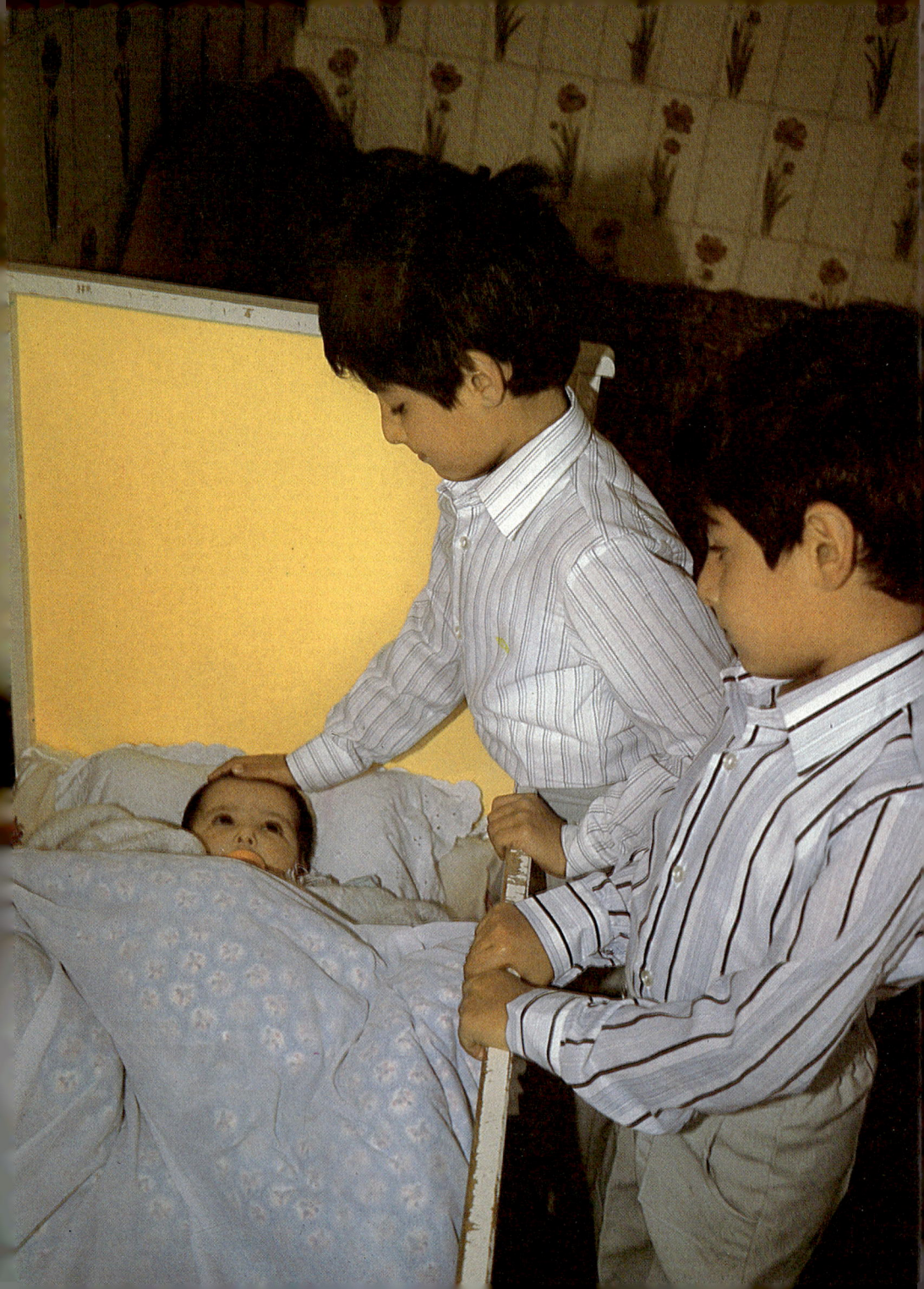

When the twins were dressed they went to see their baby sister.

"Wake up," said Qadir.

"Utho," said Imran.

Then they went downstairs and sat at the table for their breakfast.

"Do you want cornflakes this morning?" Mum asked.

"Yes please," said Qadir.

"Ji hān," said Imran.

"Dad will be home soon," said Mum. "Do you want another cup of tea?"

"No thank you," said Qadir.

"Nahe shukria," said Imran.

Just then Dad came home from work.

"Hello Imran. Hello Qadir," he said. "I want you to do a job for me."

"On your way to the mosque this morning, take this video to your uncle," said Dad. "He will give you a new one."

"The mosque!" said Qadir. "I'd forgotten."

"Masjid!" said Imran. "Men bhool gia thha."

Imran and Qadir took the video to their uncle.

"Here you are," said Qadir.

"Ye lijie," said Imran.

"And here is a new one for you," said their uncle.

On the way to the mosque Qadir and Imran stopped.

"Mum and Dad and Uncle didn't say anything about me talking in Urdu," said Imran.

"No, but you are talking in English now," laughed Qadir.

Can you read what Qadir and Imran said?

It is written in Urdu too.

Good morning
salām alakum سلام علیکم

Wake up
utho اُٹھو

Yes please
Ji hān جی ہاں

No thank you
Nahe shukria

نہیں۔ شکریہ

Mosque
Masjid

مسجد

Here you are
Ye lijie

یہ لیجیے

Also by Peter C Heaslip

The Terraced House Books

First published in Great Britain 1985
by Methuen Children's Books Ltd
11 New Fetter Lane, London EC4P 4EE
Copyright © Peter Heaslip
Printed in Great Britain
by E. T. Heron (Print) Ltd, Witham, Essex
ISBN 0 423 51430 X (net)
      0 412 51310 9 (non net)